HOW TO MAKE BIG MONEY IN THE FLEA MARKET BUSINESS

BY MOE FOSTER

a BlackWyrm book
Louisville, Kentucky

HOW TO MAKE BIG MONEY IN THE FLEA MARKET BUSINESS

A BlackWyrm Book
BlackWyrm Publishing
10307 Chimney Ridge Ct, Louisville, KY 40299

Printed in the United States of America.

Edited by Steven S. Long

ISBN: 978-1-61318-126-3

INTRODUCTION

These days it seems like you can find flea markets just about everywhere. They're popping up in stores that have gone out of business, strip malls fallen on hard times, and just about anyplace else enough people can get together to sell and buy things. You can find nearly anything for sale in flea markets if you look around enough — clothing, guns, tires, books, tools, kitchen items, DVDs, and plenty more.

Seeing how busy flea markets are, and how much unused stuff they have in their houses, a lot of people think, "Hey, maybe I could make money with a flea market booth!". Since you're reading this book, I'll bet that's what you're thinking. And you're right, you can make money selling in flea markets... provided you know what you're doing and don't make too many mistakes.

That's where this book comes in. *How To Make Money In The Flea Market Business* is a brief, fact-filled guide to the basics of creating and running a flea market booth. It'll get you on the right track so you start earning money right away instead of wasting it trying things that don't work.

I've divided *How To Make Money In The Flea Market Business* into five sections. "Choosing Your First Booth" discusses the things you should consider when deciding what sort of booth to create, and which flea market to set it up in. "Flea Market Staff" provides some tips and suggestions on how to deal with the people who run the flea market. "Building Your Booth And Displaying Your Goods" provides in-depth information on how to construct your booth, what sort of lighting and fixtures to use, and how to display the items you have for sale to attract the maximum amount of customers at the minimum risk. It includes numerous photographs to provide examples of what I'm talking about. "What You're Selling" offers some suggestions and information about specific types of goods you might sell, like clothes, firearms, and toys. The final section, "Booth Maintenance," goes over how to take care of or move your booth.

Everything I discuss in *How To Make Money In The Flea Market Business* is something I've experienced. When I started running a flea market booth people wouldn't tell me what I needed to know and do to succeed, so I had to learn on my own. Reading this book will keep you from making all the mistakes most people make — I've made them for you. *How To Make Money In The Flea Market Business* reveals everything I've learned in the business so you can use that knowledge to make money right away!

GETTING STARTED

The first question you should ask yourself is, "Why do I want to open a flea market booth?" There are many reasons to open a flea market booth, and you should make sure you understand your motivations so you get off on the right foot.

First, there's the money. People believe vendors make thousands of dollars in the flea market business. That's possible, but you shouldn't expect high earnings right off the bat. *A flea market booth is like any other business: the more you put into it the more you'll get out of it.* It's often said that "it takes money to make money," and that's as true for a flea market booth as for any other business. If you expect to get rich quick, you need to think again.

Second, there's the enjoyment of it. If you want to get into a business to have a lot of fun, running a flea market booth is it. Flea markets attract a lot of interesting people, from your fellow vendors to your customers. The process of buying and selling can be exciting, even addictive.

Third, it's a great way to sell your personal stuff. You can turn your leftovers and junk into money!

However, there are some things you should be aware of before you get into this. The flea market business will take a lot of your time and effort. It will also take a lot of gas, and put a lot of wear and tear on your car or truck. Inevitably you'll lose money on items that you know are worth more than you can get.

You'll also need a thick skin. People will steal from you, lie to you, mislead you, switch tags on your items, and look for other ways to cheat you. They'll want to sell you their items for prices that are much higher than you can re-sell them for. The cheaper you buy, the cheaper you can sell, and thus the more customers you'll have, so it's crucial not to pay too much no matter what a seller says to you. Telling people that their items aren't worth what they want for them is very difficult in the beginning, but the longer you work the flea markets the better you'll get at it.

Despite these problems, all it takes is buying an item for a real cheap price and discovering it's worth ten times what you paid for it. Then you're hooked... and looking for the next big find. It gets in your blood if you stay involved with flea markets long enough. Many of my friends have garages full of stuff they bought and just can't get in their booths — not only are their booths already full, so are their trucks!

CHOOSING YOUR FIRST BOOTH

Before you can sell things from your flea market booth you have to find a flea market with space available, and then select the space that's most suited to your budget and what you have to offer. These days many flea markets are held in stores that have gone out of business.

Here's a list of some things to consider. Many of them are discussed in greater detail later in this book.

1. Find a flea market that's close to where you live. This will save you a lot of money in gas and time.

2. Make sure the building is clean. The booths area should be uncluttered, swept on a regular basis, and have scheduled trash pick-up, but look beyond that to the rest of the facility. For example, go to the restroom and see how clean it is. If it's so filthy you wouldn't use it, leave that flea market and find another one — if you won't use it your customers won't either, which means they'll stop coming to the market.

3. Spend some time in the flea market at different times of the day, and on both weekdays and weekends, to see how busy the place is. Are there usually customers walking around, examining what's for sale in the booths, and buying things? That's the sort of flea market you want to be a part of, one that's active and positive. On the other hand, if the market usually isn't very busy, you shouldn't set up a booth there — you won't change the situation and you'll go broke.

4. After you've determined the market is clean enough and busy enough for you, see how friendly the staff is. Did they greet you when you came in? Were they sitting down at the counter, or standing up, eager to assist customers? Could you hear them talking about people as they leave the store? These people are going to be helping your customers, so you need them to behave professionally.

5. Once you're satisfied that the facility and the staff are good enough, ask the staff about renting a booth. Here are the main things to think about:
    - What does it cost to rent booth space at this flea market?
    - What rental terms are available? Be careful not to get locked into a long lease until you know you've found a market that works well for you. Most flea markets will rent you booth space on a month to month lease. This is good for both parties... but it can also be bad. A monthly lease makes it easy for you to leave if you decide you don't like the market, but it also makes it easy for the market to get rid of you.

- What size booth spaces are available? Some flea markets have different sizes of booths. Depending on what you're going to sell you may want a smaller or larger booth, if you can get one. Cost may be a factor here too; the larger booth spaces usually have a higher rent.

- Which spaces within the flea market are currently available? You want some ability to choose a booth space that's right for you and what you intend to sell. Don't take the only one left unless it's *exactly* what you're looking for — there's a reason nobody wanted the last spot in the market. On the other hand, if there's *too* much choice — a lot of booth vacancies — that probably means sales at that market aren't very good and you should look elsewhere.

- Does the booth have electricity, or at least access to it? Even if you don't think you'll need it right away, eventually you *will* want it. You'll try to sell a TV, a lamp, a radio, a clock, or something else customers will want to plug in to see if it works. If they can't test it, they won't buy it. Or you may simply want to use a small fan to keep yourself cool while you work.

- What's the lighting like? Stand in the middle of the booth space you're considering and look up so you can see where the lights are. Will your booth space be well-lit or dim? This will make a lot of difference when you work there all day, particularly when there are lots of customers in your booth. Ideally you want a light source that's right above your booth but that doesn't glare. (See "Lighting" later in this book for more ideas.)

- Can you put up walls, and if so how tall can they be? Can you use wood studs or metal studs? (Some states require you to use metal studs. Find out about this before you buy all the supplies you'll need to build your walls.)

- What sort of neighbors will you have? Look at the booths next to and near the space you're thinking about. Are they clean or messy? What do they sell? Will they go well with your booth or make you look bad? Are they competing with you directly? You don't want to put your booth up near messy booths, booths that won't get much traffic, booths that are selling things that smell or make noise, or booths that are selling exactly the sorts of things you want to sell.

You probably won't find a *perfect* booth space, at least not right away, but you shouldn't settle for a space that makes your job harder. If you can't find a booth space you like, maybe you should wait one more month and see what opens up. Get on the market's waiting list. If it doesn't have a waiting list, ask yourself why. Is it because no one wants to rent booth space there, or because the staff is disorganized? Either reason is a good indication you should find a better market to sell at.

FLEA MARKET STAFF

A professionally-run flea market should have a staff. These people show booths to prospective customers, help customers find your booth, maintain the common areas, deal with disputes among vendors, and handle all the other matters that individual booth owners like you can't or shouldn't.

You want the members of the staff to be your friends. They're the ones who take care of your things while you're not there. They don't clean your booth or straighten it up, but they watch so no one steals your items. They can't see everything going on, of course — but if they like you they'll keep a closer eye on your booth. So, make yourself known. Learn their names. Learn what they like. Give them a discount on items they like. Share your doughnuts. They'll return the favor.

Your customers are the staff's customers too. They'll direct them to your booth if they like you, so besides making them like you, make sure they know what you're selling. That way when a customer asks for your items the staff knows where to send him. After all, while some people come to a flea market to stroll the aisles and look for deals, others only have a little time and want to go directly to what they're looking for. On the other hand, if you're causing problems or giving the staff a hard time, they won't send any potential buyers your way.

The staff members know if there are other booth spaces becoming available that you might want. If they're aware you're looking for a better location in the market or a bigger spot, they'll let you know first if they like you. Naturally they'd prefer to give a good location to a friendly vendor with an established track record rather than a new vendor. If you get along well with the staff they'll also loan you tools when you need them, let you know if another vendor has an item you're looking for, and provide all sorts of other help.

One of the staff's most important jobs is to check vendors whenever they takes things out of the flea market — especially at the end of the month when some vendors are moving out. The staff should check everything from every vendor when it leaves the store. Most vendors are honest but some aren't, and of course anyone can make a mistake from time to time, so having someone check on what's being taken out of the market is crucial.

The best thing about good flea market staff is that they know what an item should cost, most of the time. If a customer brings up an item and the price seems too cheap, a good counter person pays attention. He catches mistakes — and tag switchers.

Most flea market staff people get paid by the hour, and usually it's just minimum wage. It can be a hard job, especially when they have to deal with negative behavior by customers, kids, and vendors. Make their lives easier by not being a problem for them — it will pay off every time. After all, most of the time they want to help you. If they don't care about you or your booth then you're in trouble.

BUILDING YOUR BOOTH

Once you've selected the space for your booth, you have to build the booth itself. This may be as simple as setting up tables and racks, or as complex as constructing your own walls and shelving. And of course the main thing to keep in mind as you plan and build your booth is how you want to display the goods you'll have for sale.

Booth Size

The booth sizes available vary from flea market to flea market, often based on the amount of floor space in the building where the market's held. In most flea markets the normal booth size is 8 feet by 10 feet, or 10 feet by 10 feet. Some markets have one-and-a-half size spaces, or offer a block of booth spaces. Check with the staff and get pricing for all the options that interest you before you make your final decision.

In most flea markets a booth can be as tall as eight feet. That's really all you'll need — if you go any higher than that customers will have to climb around in your booth, which means they'll knock things over and may get hurt.

Usually you should start out with just one booth. After you've worked the flea market for awhile you may find that it's not for you (and give up flea marketing entirely), or you may discover that you need more booth space to display all the stuff you want to sell. If you want to expand, tell the staff about your plans and see if they can find you an available booth space near your first booth — or better yet, right next to it so you can combine them into one big booth. If you have booths across the market from one another you're going to waste a lot of time going back and forth between them, moving items from one to the other, and so on. You may even have to hire someone to help you run them, which cuts into your profits.

Arranging Your Booth

How you arrange your booth is important. If you put a showcase in front you're showing off your best items to everyone... but you may make it harder for people to get into your booth to see the rest of your goods, or the case may become a "barrier" that prevents you from interacting with your customers. If you set up your shelves so that customers can't move around inside your booth easily, you'll cost yourself sales. A lot of this is common sense stuff once you think about it, but you should think about it *before* you set things up and make mistakes.

The main thing to consider is this: do you want a "walk through" booth or a "side by side" booth? In a walk through booth, the customers come in one end and can walk around, exiting either out the other end or through the way they came in. Typically small items are displayed on peg boards along the walls, with shelves or tables in the middle. If you create a walk through booth, be sure to leave enough room for people to push shopping carts (if carts are available in your flea market) — if a customer can't get his cart into your booth he often won't go in at all.

A side by side booth has two or more booths arranged as one large, open display space (possibly with shelves or racks along the back wall). It's ideal for furniture and similar large items.

Some other tips: don't block the front of your booth. Put bright things in the front to draw attention. Make your booth as homey and inviting as possible.

Other Considerations

Sometimes it's possible to get a booth space next to one of the walls of the building the flea market's held in. This can be to your advantage if you want to hang flags or banners, put up big pictures or posters, and so on. For example, I've seen a vendor who put a big clock ten feet above his booth to attract attention.

It's often a good idea to get a booth space close to the restrooms. Everyone needs to go to the restroom before he leaves or when he comes into the flea market. Being near the break area or the concession stand is a good place for similar reasons.

Remember to use all the space you can get for your money. If it's not obvious where the boundaries of your booth are, ask the staff so you can be sure; this will prevent problems with your neighbors.

Lighting

In many flea markets the overhead lights are so far away that they don't give your booth the lighting it needs. In that case you should supply your own.

The type of lighting you need depends entirely on how you arrange your booth and what you're selling. Some items require better lighting to see properly; if your customers can't examine them carefully under good lighting you'll lose sales. Spend a little time in the lighting department at Lowe's or Home Depot and you should be able to find lots of good ways to light your booth.

Lamps

Lamps give your booth a homey feeling — the familiar illumination attracts people so they come into your booth to see what you're selling. Floor lamps and table lamps usually qualify as props (items you use but that are also for sale; see below), so make sure you don't sell all your lighting away! Always tag your lamps, even if they're not for sale — and if they're not, make sure they're clearly marked that way so people don't ask you about them.

Depending on how you run your booth, you may want to put timers on your lamps so that they're only on during market hours. They only cost a few dollars at most hardware and department stores and save you money on bulbs in the long run.

Overhead Lights

There are plenty of possibilities for hanging and overhead lighting if you're willing to do a little work installing it. This assumes, of course, that you have walls and a ceiling to hang them from. Often you can attach a board to the top of your walls and put the lighting fixture on it; that way you don't lose valuable display space for the lighting fixture. If you do this, try to put the board as close to the electrical outlet as possible.

Track lights often make good lighting for flea market booths. You can direct the light where you want it, making it easy to adjust the lighting if you re-arrange your booth. And they're not the sort of thing that's normally for sale so you won't get a lot of questions about them.

If you have a ceiling, you could use standard 4 foot long fluorescent lights. They should be in the middle of your booth if at all possible. The bulbs last a long time and can be purchased at hardware stores along with the lights. However, they may seem a bit too "institutional" to some customers compared to lamps or other types of hanging lights.

Cords

Be careful about the cords for lighting (and any other electrical devices you use, for that matter). If they're out where people can see them, it looks messy. Even worse, someone may trip over them and get hurt, or accidentally pull them out of the wall. If possible, keep the cords concealed under or behind tables, shelves, and other booth fixtures.

You should also take care not to overload your booth with too many cords, which is a fire risk. It's easy to do, particularly if you only have one electrical outlet in your booth, so you have to pay attention and use the proper equipment. For example, always try to get lighting that has cords with three prongs.

If your lighting's not working, there are a few things you should check. First see if the bulb's burned out. If that doesn't seem to be the case, see if someone's unplugged your light. This will happen frequently if customers can see your electrical outlets. They'll unplug your things and use your outlet to test something, then forget to plug your lamp back in. And if the item they're testing doesn't work, they may just leave it there.

Walls

Not all flea market booths have walls, but most do because they allow you to use all the space you're paying for. You can only fit so many tables into a booth space — creating and using walls effectively lets you display more goods for sale. Anything you can hang on the walls gives you more room for other things elsewhere.

If possible you should create your own walls rather than using the back side of the walls erected by your neighbors. For one thing, your neighbors might not like it if you use their walls. But more importantly, if a neighbor takes down or re-arranges a wall you're using, that will cause problems for you. Better to have your own walls and avoid those problems.

Of course, when building your walls, be sure to stay inside the space allotted to you. This will save you from having to take down a wall that's larger than your space.

PEGBOARD WALLS

Making walls out of pegboard is usually your best bet. White pegboard comes in the right size: four foot wide by eight foot tall sheets. That's about as high as you can realistically go without causing problems for yourself and your customers. If you have higher walls, customers won't be able to reach some items easily, and they'll knock things down and tear up your booth trying to get them. The 4 x 8 foot sections are easy for you to move or re-arrange if necessary.

What makes pegboard so great for your booth's walls is that the flexibility of the peg system allows you to easily adjust how you display items, move them around, and so on. You can obtain pegs for them at hardware stores, home improvement stores, and the like; sometimes other vendors in the flea market will carry them for even cheaper prices. But you can also use hooks, which come in sizes from 1 to 12 inches. Choose the size that best suits what you want to display.

SLAT WALLS

A slat wall sort of a newer version of pegboard. It has slat lines in it and uses a different kind of hook.

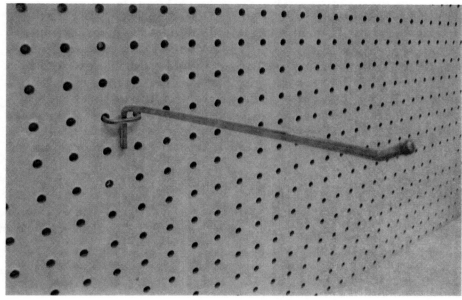

a pegboard wall

Slat walls are a little more expensive and sometimes a little harder to find than pegboard, and they're much heavier as well, but they have some advantages too. Instead of taking out a peg in your pegboard you just slide the slat wall hook over to where you need it. Slat walls are also easier to paint and you can adjust them to your liking.

a slat wall

LATTICE WALLS

Some flea market booths have walls made of latticework (white or natural). They look good to some people, but they're not practical for most flea market items. They're harder to work with, hanging things on them is usually more difficult than on pegboard, and you can see right through them. If you're selling flowers, plants, and similar items, lattice walls may be the way to go, but for most items pegboard works better. However, for some booths it's possible to put lattice on top of them to hang things from. (Just be careful this doesn't block the light and darken your booth too much.)

DRYWALL AND PANELING

You can also use ordinary drywall or paneling to construct your booth walls, but usually this isn't a good idea. They're heavy, hard to work with, and hard to hang things from. They lack the flexibility of pegboard as well. On the other hand they're very sturdy, so if you know you're going to stay in the same booth space, with the same booth arrangement and booth display, for a long time, they're worth considering.

BUILDING YOUR OWN WALLS

Of course, you can build your own walls out of plywood or anything that you like, if you prefer — it's not as hard as you might think.

I like to build the frame on the ground first. I take an eight foot long 2x4 and cut it in half — one half for the top of the frame, one for the bottom. Use two more eight-foot 2x4s for the sides, giving you a frame that's 48 inches (4 feet) wide and 96 inches (8 feet) tall. you'll need three more four-foot 2x4s ("studs") to put in the middle of the framework to brace it. Fasten all this together with three-inch screws. When the frame's complete, attach your pegboard (or whatever you're using) to it with one-inch screws.

You build additional frames the same way, but you may have to attach them to the first frame before putting the pegboard on. You do this with 3½-inch screws, and should also stabilize them by attaching another 2x4 across the top of both (and sometimes one on the corners as well).

Here's a list of the materials I use to build a typical booth. This information is based on prices in my area in 2008, so you should check stores in your own area for the most current information before making any firm estimates.

Of course, that list just covers materials. You also need a truck to carry it all (or buy it from a place that delivers it where you need it), and you'll have to hire someone to do the work if you don't have the time, tools, and desire to do it yourself. (Even if you do, having a second person to help you makes the job a lot easier.)

Wall-Building Estimate	
Nine sheets of 4' x 8' pegboard:	$144.00
Nine 8-foot long 2x4s:	$22.00
27 studs:	$58.00
Two 10-foot 2x4s:	$5.00
70 3" screws:	$10.00
144 1' drywall screws:	$10.00
Total Estimated Cost:	**$249.00**

SELLING YOUR WALLS WHEN YOU'RE DONE

Sometimes you can get back most of the money you spent on walls when you leave a flea market for good. Another vendor — either an existing one or a new one who's taking over your spot — may need them. The staff may be able to sell your walls for you. You won't get full price for them, but you'll recover part of your cost and save the time and effort you'd otherwise have to spend moving the walls.

Wheels

If you re-arrange your booth a lot, or move things between booths, putting wheels on your shelves, props, fixtures, and furniture can be extremely helpful — it's easier on the items and on your back! Just make sure that the wheels (or wheeled items you buy) are sturdy enough for what you need to display.

You can buy wheels at your local hardware or home improvement store. You can usually attach them with four screws apiece, and of course you usually need four wheels per item. This can get a little expensive, but it's well worth the cost for the time and effort it will save you in the long run.

If you can't (or don't want to) put wheels on an item (maybe because you want to sell it), you can use a furniture mover instead. These are sturdy wheeled platforms built of 2x4s that you put under a heavy item so you can move it easily; movers use them all the time. You can make your own with just a few minutes' effort. Be sure to put your name and vendor number on your furniture mover; otherwise someone might claim it's theirs.

DISPLAYING YOUR GOODS
Shelving

Many people don't think about it at first when planning to create a flea market booth, but shelving is a crucial issue. You can't sell an item if you can't show it to the customers, and shelves are the primary way you do that in many types of booths.

As you think about what type of shelves to get, consider the issue of space. Space is limited in a booth, and you pay just as much for the space you don't use (or waste) as you do for the space you use. For example, if you're selling small items, shelves that are placed too far apart are wasting space (though you should always make sure there's room for customers to pick up and examine a small object easily). Shelving that allows you to adjust the height of the individual shelves can really help cut down on unused space.

If possible, attach your shelves to the walls of your booth. That makes the whole structure sturdier and ensures that a shelf won't accidentally fall on someone. Sometimes it's also possible to attach shelves to one another.

PLASTIC SHELVES

Plastic shelves are the most common these days. If they're not adjustable you may be able to cut them down to fit whatever you're selling, or to make all the shelves in the booth uniform. (Neatness always looks more appealing to the customer.) However, some plastic shelving can be a little on the flimsy side — put bigger and heavier items on the bottom if possible.

WOOD SHELVES

Wood shelves — often in the form of bookcases — are readily available, but may not work well for your booth. They're heavy and hard to move around. They're often hard (or sometimes impossible) to adjust, which may mean wasted space. But they tend to be durable and sturdy, making them good for holding large or heavy items.

METAL AND WIRE SHELVES

A lot of vendors use metal shelves in their flea market booths, but I tend to stay away from them. They're not always as strong as they look, often need painting, and can be hard to adjust. On the other hand, wire shelves that hang easily on walls are often good for small items like DVDs and CDs.

GLASS SHELVES

With so many big stores going out of business around town, flea market vendors have been buying up glass shelving units for good prices. However, just because they look good doesn't mean they're a good idea for your booth. They're pretty and flashy at first... but they show all the dust in the store. The less time you have to spend dusting and cleaning, the better.

Glass shelves could also be dangerous. With the metal carts in some markets and kids running around, things get knocked over and glass shelves can get broken. So if you want to use glass shelves, be careful about where you place them and what you put on them.

GONDOLA SHELVES

If you have more than two booths *gondola shelving* is good to have. You see these sorts of shelves in grocery stores and some other commercial establishments. They're usually sturdy, made of metal, have adjustable shelves that can hold a lot of items (and can be cleaned with soap and water). The typical one is about four to six feet high. They're heavy, so put them somewhere you can leave them for a long time.

SAFEGUARDING YOUR SHELVES

Smaller shelves, particularly small wooden bookcases and other types that are found around the home, are attractive to customers. If you can't firmly attach them to your walls, make sure to label them (and any removable parts) "Not For Sale" and with your name and vendor number (if any). Otherwise, sooner or later a customer will take everything off a shelf you don't want to sell, bring it to the sales counter, and want to buy it. It might not make it back to your booth.

Showcases

Besides shelves (see above) and tables (see below), another way to display the things you're selling is a showcase (also called a display case). If you want to sell small, valuable items (watches, jewelry, coins, stamps...) or dangerous things (handguns, knives...), you need one. If you leave things like that out in your booth where anyone can touch them, they'll be stolen.

Unless you have enough items to fill a whole showcase, don't worry about getting one at first. Worry about setting up your booth, getting your business running, and finding the items to fill the showcase. (After all, a half-full showcase won't draw much attention.) Once you've got enough showcase items, then you can get a showcase for your booth. (Of course, if you know you're planning to have a showcase eventually, plan your booth arrangement so you can easily add one.)

Showcases can be expensive — and the better shape they're in, the higher the cost. If a piece of glass is broken the showcase is worth much less... but you'll have to pay for new glass, and pay someone to install it. So unless you're going to be in the flea market business a long time, don't buy an expensive showcase for your goods.

Some flea markets rent showcases to vendors. Renting may mean less expense and fewer headaches for you in the long run.

SHOWCASE TYPES AND FEATURES

Showcases come in many sizes and shapes. Typically the kind you want for a flea market booth are from three to seven feet long, and three to seven feet tall — any bigger than that and they may not fit well (and are difficult to move). An "average" showcase is probably four feet tall and four to five feet long... but they come in all sizes.

I prefer a five foot long showcase with all glass in the front and three shelves inside. However, there are tall cases which are mostly glass, allowing you to display your goods well — you want the customer to see as much of an item as he can, since the more he can see the greater the chance he'll become interested and buy it.

When buying a showcase, consider whether it's the type you fill from the front or from the back. This affects where you can put the showcase. One that loads from the back can't be put against a wall, so it will have to take up valuable floor space. On the other hand, a front-loader usually has to be placed against a wall, which prevents you from hanging anything on that part of your wall.

You should balance the attractiveness of the glass in a showcase against the usefulness of the case. In some cases the more glass a showcase has, the fewer items it can hold. Don't buy one based just on how it looks — figure out what you need in terms of storage space, then find a showcase that fits the bill *and* is attractive.

If possible, get a showcase that has lighting. The bulbs are a little on the expensive side, but the lighting shows off your products much better. Similarly, some cases have a mirrored back. This is also a good feature if it doesn't add too much to the price and the mirror isn't broken.

LOCKS

Another feature you should pay attention to is the lock on a showcase. Most come with an installed lock, but over the years the keys get lost or the lock broken. Make sure the case you're considering has a working lock with keys.

Many vendors use a slide lock that's easily put on glass doors to keep them from opening. However, in many cases these locks aren't very secure. A better idea, if the doors aren't made of glass, is to put a hasp on them and use a padlock. This doesn't look as good, but it's harder for a thief to get into a showcase that's padlocked.

WHERE TO PUT YOUR SHOWCASE

If you have a choice, you may not want to put your showcase in your booth. In many cases there won't even be enough room for it! Even a 2' x 4' case takes up a lot of floor space in an 8' x 10' booth. Depending on whether a case is front-loading or back-loading there may only be specific places within your booth that you can put it, even if that interferes with your other booth arrangement plans.

Vendors who have showcases in their booth often have to put them near the front. This may block customers' access to the rest of the booth. It also lets a thief hide what he's trying to steal. (Particularly if he works with a partner — they can get into the case in seconds while no one's looking, and it may be days before you even realize anything's been taken.) If you put a showcase in your booth this will happen to you, sooner or later.

A better approach, if possible, is to place your showcase at the front of the flea market building and let the counter staff watch over it and handle the sales for you. This will cost you some money — the flea market staff rents that showcase space to vendors, they don't give it away — but it's worth it to free up space in your booth and cut down on theft.

Tables

The easiest way to display your goods is on tables. The first thing many new vendors want to do is get a table and put some things on it.

Tables are often the best way to go for your booth: they come in all possible shapes and sizes; they can hold a lot of goods; and they don't require you to do any construction work or invest a lot of money. If you cover them with a decorative cloth you can store things under them without customers seeing it and thinking that your booth is a mess. (On the other hand, doing this may deprive you of space under the table where you could display some items.)

But tables also have their downsides. They occupy a lot of space and may not be the most efficient way of using that space. As customers pick up and examine your goods your tables can become disorganized and messy pretty quickly, particularly if your booth is on a corner or end cap (or if you've put the table at the front of your booth). And people will walk by with something they really don't want and lay it down on the first empty space they can find — your table. In my experience, before long you'll want to get rid of your tables and buy more shelving.

a typical folding table

Here's a picture of a typical folding table, the kind that might go in the front of your booth for a short time. Most of them are about the same size. When you don't need them you can fold them up and easily store them behind a cabinet or shelf. They're handy for quick sale items, but they're not very stable. Don't put tall items on one — if someone bumps it, everything might fall and break.

This table is a little longer. It also folds, but due to its size it's harder to hide when not in use. On the other hand, you can make it look good with a table cloth and then store things underneath it.

a longer folding table

Props

"Props" is a general term for items you use to display the things you're selling, but which may also be for sale themselves. For example, a china cabinet is a good way to display glassware and dishes, and mannequins are ideal for clothing booths. Other props include quilt racks, TV stands, curio cabinets, coffee tables, end tables, corner cabinets/shelves, plate racks, old crates and barrels, old iron headboards and footboards, room dividers, and cedar chests.

If you want to sell a prop as well as what it displays, you have to decide how badly you want to sell it — a prop may have more value for you as a display piece. In that case you can put such a high price on the prop that it's unlikely anyone will ever buy it... and if someone does anyway, you make more than enough money to buy another prop while still putting some cash in your pocket. On the other hand, if you want to re-arrange your booth and have to get rid of some props, you can price them to move knowing you've already gotten your money's worth out of them as display pieces.

Look in some home decorating books and magazines and you'll get plenty of ideas for clever, creative ways to display your goods. For example, one time I found two saddles and made a horse and Derby display. The saddles were the main theme and people came over just to see them. I had a Derby print and some Derby glasses for sale in the booth. The saddles actually sold too fast because they're usually not found in flea markets and someone thought they looked good in the display. But if you're going to complain about your booth, "things are selling too quickly" is about the best complaint you can have.

Depending on what you're selling you can choose props and decor to create a theme. For example, in my booth where I sell old records I have musical instruments — drums, horns, guitars — and instrument cases hanging from the ceiling; I also staple old album covers to the walls. It looks cool and people comment on it all the time.

Price Labels

Before you can sell your goods you have to put a price on them — and customers have to be able to find out what it is quickly and easily, particularly if it's the sort of flea market where you're not there to work your booth. That means you have to use price labels, or tags.

In some flea markets the staff sells price tags to vendors as a service — a very helpful service when you've forgotten your tags or bought something on your way to work in your booth. If the market doesn't carry them, ask the staff to. After all, you're their customer.

WHAT TO PUT ON PRICE LABELS

First and foremost, of course, you have to say what the item's price is. But you should also put your booth number/vendor number (or some other identifying statement) on every price label. In fact, some flea markets may require that you do this — the staff may not be allowed to take money for any items that don't have a vendor tag. Customers get angry when they want to buy something and the staff won't let them... and lost customers are rarely a good thing.

If there's room on the tag, put a brief description of the item. This takes time, but it makes it a lot harder for dishonest customers to switch tags. (I like to use a big label and then put a piece of packaging tape on it. That makes it even more difficult for someone to try to switch the tag.) If the flea market staff handles sales, the description helps them ensure the right item's being sold.

I also use a black felt tip pin to put my vendor number on the bottom or back of furniture and other big items in case another vendor tries to say the item's his. Always identify your products before you leave the flea market — if you don't someone else might. And that's how some vendors get out of the store with items that don't belong to them. Not all vendors are honest, unfortunately.

TYPES OF LABELS

Price labels come in many sizes and shapes, so you have plenty of options to choose from to suit your goods and booth the best.

For many booths and items the traditional yard sales labels work just fine. They come in many colors and are very noticeable. You can buy them at your local Wal-mart or K-mart stores and other places. Specialized dealers may also have things like plate holders, signs, and ring and necklace holders.

Some price tags come with strings on them to tie to a leg or hole in an item. They're a little more expensive. They come in different sizes too.

Another way to label your items is to write the price on a regular piece of paper. Using large letters, and/or colored letters, draws attention to what you're trying to sell. If you're good at crafts you can even use colored paper, cutouts, and so on — like scrapbooking. But of course, a price label that large only works well on larger items, like furniture, or when one price applies to a lot of items ("Anything In This Bin $1 Apiece!").

For some types of booths you should consider investing in a tagging gun. A tagging gun pokes a hole in fabric or other items with a two or three inch plastic tie — just like what big stores often use to attach price labels to clothing. They're very handy and often cheap (less than $20).

PRICE GUNS

If you have many small items that are alike you'll use a lot of small tags, and in that case you might want to consider a price gun. These devices shoot out a pre-printed price label really fast, thus making your job a little easier and quicker. However, you may not be able to include any information but the price, and the tags come off easily, making those items a target for tag switchers.

You can buy price guns and the labels for them at stores like Office Depot or online. They're not cheap — often well over $100 for a good model, though refurbished models are less expensive — but they're worth it in the long run if you price a lot of items. Make sure you buy a two-line gun; that way you can include both the price and your booth/vendor number. I prefer the Monarch guns, such as the Monarch 1136.

When you have a price gun, take good care of it — they're made of plastic and break easily if you step on them or drop something on them. And if you put it down, watch it carefully, because a dishonest vendor or customer might steal it. I try to put my gun in a high place, like on top of a shelf or bookcase, so it's not easy for anyone to reach.

a pricing gun

EXAMPLES

Here are some pictures of some of the things I talked about above.

Cabinets like this aren't typically used as showcases although I have seen some that were. Some people use them for displaying glassware; they show off your items nicely. Some of them have built-in lights, too. You should put cabinets like these against the wall so they won't fall on anyone — sometimes the doors stick, and if someone pulls on them too hard the cabinet will fall forward if it's not against the wall.

cabinetry

On the next page is a picture of a double booth — it displays well and is easy to get into (or you can stand in the aisle and see things of interest). It's full; the vendor's using most of the wall space.

The next booth looks good, but you can see how lattice walls make it harder to display pictures neatly. There's lots of wasted space. If you're using lattice walls, vines might look good somewhere close to the top for decoration. Notice the boards on the top of the walls holding the walls together.

Count the items in this booth and see how much wasted space there is. By installing two bookcases in this booth the vendor could put all the items on the tables in the cases, giving him an entire wall and lots of floor space to add more goods. The vendor isn't even using the display area under the tables (he probably used it for storage, thus costing himself selling space).

double booth

lattice booth

This is a corner booth, probably four to five booths altogether. It looks homey and is easy to get into without a cart. The items in this booth are expensive, the sort you should display with plenty of room. Notice the border across the top of the booths. Also notice the picture prop that's holding the unframed prints.

corner booth

This booth is cluttered and hard to get into. It appears to be a double booth where the vendor's trying to use all the space he has, but he's gone a little too far. The short walls in the front hide what's in the back, which also creates a breeding ground for thieves. It would be hard to get a shopping cart in this booth. If someone's already in there another customer's not likely to go in.

cluttered booth

Below is a table sunglass rack. There are many kinds of racks for glasses. When they're new, they're expensive, but if you can buy one from a vendor who's getting out of this line of business or at an auction you may get a good price. However, you shouldn't use this sort of rack for expensive or highly desirable sunglasses; people will steal them. Put those in your showcase and save this rack for cheaper merchandise.

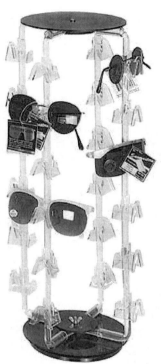

sunglass rack   *earring display*

To its right is a table earring display. This one doesn't rotate, but some do; in either case they're not very expensive (sometimes as cheap as $12-15). There are also floor models. If you have only a few earrings a tabletop one works fine; if you're selling a lot of jewelry a floor model or some sort of hanging display on your wall might be better.

Small items like earrings are easy to steal. Keep them in a well-lit space and as out in the open as possible. Keep more expensive jewelry in a showcase.

This is a slat wall tower. You can use one of these for jewelry and just about any other small item. This style has wheels and four sides; you should put it in the middle of your floor space, not against a wall. The longer the pegs you use, the more open space you need around the tower — people will bump into them and knock them off the slats if you don't give them plenty of room to move around.

Slat wall towers aren't cheap — they cost $50 or more depending on size, condition, and other factors. Sometimes you can get lucky and find a jewelry store or other retailer who's remodeling and will get rid of them for a good price.

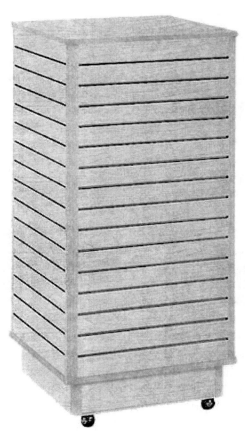

slat wall tower

This is a picture of some banana boxes. The top layer is the only box that has items in it. The boxes on the bottom are just there to provide some height. Look at the wasted space! No walls, no effort, very little investment in making the booth a good place to shop. The boxes are also a "collect-all" for customers who'll throw things in them that they've decided not to buy. A lot of the things in this booth could be hung up and displayed for a customer to view.

banana boxes

Here's a record booth in one of my flea markets. Notice the description on the front of the boxes that tells you what type of records are in each box. As you can see, the boxes aren't full; this gives customers room to flip through the albums and see the covers without anything getting damaged. (You should also do this with things like magazines and comic books, though you may have to take precautions so they don't warp or get bent.)

However, look above the albums and see the wasted space. One shelf has just a single row of albums; the top shelf has nothing at all. After I moved the shelves I was able to incorporate 45s and a row of candles at no extra rent. This move saved me eighty dollars in booth rental fees.

record booth with unused space

record booth reorganized for efficiency

This corner booth has no walls, so it looks empty and uninviting. I wouldn't try to finish out a booth like this — it won't make much money because there's so much empty space. The one good thing about this booth is that the vendor hasn't put out a table — as people walk past corner booths they tend to put unwanted things on tables within reach.

Also notice the metal studs on the back walls. In some states these are required instead of wood studs. Ask about this before buying material for your walls.

booth without walls

This is a tool booth. Notice how well-organized it is; there's almost no wasted space. There's a great prop — a board with peg board on the front of it to display the hats and the stop sign. There's room for a cart and for two people to be in the booth at the same time. The floor isn't cluttered and the shelves are full and neat. Most men won't walk past this booth without checking it out; they just can't help it. However, it's hard to keep a booth this neat and organized; the vendor will have to be here two or three times a week or it will become a mess.

well-organized tool booth

Cups sell well in flea markets, especially if they have a name, logo, or design people can identify with. The mirror in this picture shows off how many cups there are.

Notice the prop in the bottom left-hand corner — the trunk used to display pictures. There's a price on it, but it's so high most people won't want to disturb the display. Without a price label on it, someone might take the trunk (empty of course) to the counter to ask how much it costs, and then the booth is a wreck.

use pegboards to maximize hanging item space

Look at this booth's back wall. The vendor uses a cork board to display jewelry in little baggies clipped to the board with push pins. He puts the price tag on the back of the product so it doesn't hide the item. The mirrors make the booth look bigger. He uses the vanity in the lower right-hand corner to display makeup, scarves, and that sort of things. Some people like to root around in boxes or baskets for the treasures they might find, so you may want to display a lot of similar small items that way.

jewelry displayed on cork board with prices on back

WHAT YOU'RE SELLING

You can sell pretty much anything at most flea markets. From furniture, to clothing, collectibles, antiques, food, and just about everything in between, you can find someone selling it at some flea market somewhere. Check with the staff to learn the rules pertaining to your particular flea market, or if you have any questions about unusual or potentially dangerous items.

Here are some notes on items that may require special consideration, and other factors affecting how you operate your booth.

Clothes

Selling clothes in your booth can be a lot of work. Most people have clothes to sell, so there's lots of competition, and you need a way to display all those clothes. Hang them if you can — buy or build a strong clothes rack. If you fold them and put them on a table, as soon as a few people look through them it will all be a mess, since most people won't re-fold the clothes after looking at them (or at best fold them badly). The more orderly your clothes are, the more people will browse through them — people love to look through clothes.

Make sure all your clothes for sale are clean. Dirty clothes make your booth look bad and will cost you customers.

Clothes and related items (purses, hats, coats, and so on) are easy for people to steal. They can quickly fold them up and put them in a bag, or simply wear them out of the booth. People particularly seem to like to try on new shoes, even if they have no intention of buying them.

On the next page is a picture of some hanging clothing in a newly-built booth. It's neat and in order, but there's wasted space above the pants and below the shirts. You're paying for that space, so you should use it.

Firearms and Knives

Some flea markets have a policy against firearms. If you do sell firearms, particularly antique or rare ones, you should keep them under lock and key — a showcase is ideal for this.

You should also put any type of knife or other dangerous object in a showcase. Not only are they targets for thieves, children might play with them and hurt themselves if the knives are within easy reach.

hanging clothes in a new booth

Toys

These days toys are a hot item. They're easy to find around the house —
many people have their share of toys and would love to get rid of them.
Toys have value *if* they're clean and have all the pieces with them. (Antique
toys may have some value regardless of condition, and ones in truly good
condition, especially if they're still in the packaging, can command high
prices. These toys should be kept in a display case to prevent children — and
nostalgic adults! — from playing with them.) Otherwise they just take up
space in your booth — and the bigger the toy, the more space.

If you have toys on display, children will come in and play with them.
Sometimes they'll carry them around your booth (or the building!) and
leave them anywhere. Parents don't always buy the toys their children are
handling, or have the courtesy to make the child put the toy back where it
was — they'll let the kid drag your goods around just to keep them
occupied. And by the time a child leaves your booth after playing with
several toys, you'll have a mess to clean up. So unless you're willing to put
up with all these headaches you may want to avoid selling toys entirely.

Quilts

Quilts, blankets, comforters, and afghans are hard to display. When a customer unfolds one of these but doesn't buy it, he'll lay it back down without folding it back the way he found it, hiding all the other items for sale. He may also knock over things. In any event, your booth will look messy — and it will stay that way until you have the time and opportunity to straighten things, causing you to lose money.

The best way to avoid this problem is to hang the items up. Bundle it up and then put a zip-tie around it close to the top, and use the ziptie to hang it from a hook. When someone wants to look at it they can spread it out, and when they let go it falls back into place inside the booth.

Here's a picture of a hung quilt.

hung quilt

WHAT YOU'RE BUYING
Seasons

In my experience there's a definite seasonal cycle to sales in flea markets that you should be aware of.

In the spring, as the weather improves and people can spend more time out of doors, the flea market business suffers. Besides the fact that people have a lot of other activities to occupy their time, this is the most likely time of year for yard sales — people are cleaning out their garages and basements, and in the process competing with you for business. (However, if you have the time to shop yard sales yourself, you may find some excellent bargains you can sell for a profit in your booth later on.)

In the summertime, the situation worsens. People are either outside doing things, or they just want to stay at home where it's cool and not go outside in the heat. The kids are out of school, the pools are open, people go on vacation... and there are still yard sales. The summer's always been the least active time of year at my booths.

Things pick up after the kids go back to school, Mom can get out of the house again, and autumn arrives. Halloween, Thanksgiving, and Christmas all help to spur sales. Similarly, in the winter people prefer indoor activities — like going to the flea market to browse and buy things. In my booths I sell more items in the fall and winter than in spring and summer by a large margin. So my advice to you is, fill up your booth in the late summer or early fall so you're prepared for the strong sales period.

But just because sales are slow doesn't mean there aren't productive things you can do. The spring and summer are good times for a booth makeover! Give the place a thorough cleaning, re-arrange your displays, and so on. Don't let the time go to waste — in one way or another, time is money.

Buying Personal Property

When you work in the flea market business, people will sometimes try to sell you their personal property — things they want to get rid of for some reason.

If a potential seller wants to bring goods into the flea market for you to look at, make sure you're aware of the market's policies on this. The seller should check in with the staff — that way they know what he's bringing in, so if you decide not to buy it he can take it home without the staff giving him any trouble. If you can, you might even want to meet him at the door and explain to the staff what's going on; staying on their good side is always to your benefit.

Once the seller's through the door, try to conclude the deal up front if you can; otherwise, take him back to your booth so you can examine the items. Evaluate them and make a fair offer based on an item's desirability and condition. But keep in mind that a "fair offer" is from your perspective as a retailer. Ideally you want to at least double your money on anything you sell, so if you offer a seller more than 50% of what you think you can sell an item for you're cutting into your own profits (and may end up taking a loss once you factor in all your expenses). If you have to put in some labor cleaning the item or preparing it for display, that increases your costs and reduces the amount you can afford to offer the seller — remember, your time and effort are money!

Sometimes a seller may drive up to the flea market with a truckful of goods they want to unload quickly. In that case you have to examine them as best you can and make a decision on a price for the whole lot... and you have to have a way to get them out of the seller's vehicle into your own truck or your booth.

Beware of buying stolen goods! Obviously you don't want to do this; it can cause all sorts of problems for you. If you know the seller personally this shouldn't be a concern, but with strangers it's a definite possibility. If something doesn't seem right, or a deal's too good to be true, it's probably better for you to say "No, thanks" and walk away. You may also want to keep a record of the seller's name and contact information in case any difficulties arise later.

Buying Goods from a House

Occasionally someone will ask you to come to their house to look at and buy things. Unless you know the seller well, don't go into one of these situations alone, particularly if you're carrying a pocketful of cash — having another person along not only makes it safer for you, he can help you carry anything you buy. Even then, you have to be careful, and it helps to have a witness along. For example, I've had to return things because the husband said his wife was asleep and he was taking care of getting rid of things... but then she woke up and wanted to sue me for stealing things out of her garage.

If you're buying a whole houseful of goods (or any other large amount), don't pay for everything until you've taken out the last load; otherwise you might not get it all. Never pay up front and leave to get help or your truck — pay when you return, have loaded everything onto your truck, and are able to take it all in one load. If you have to take several loads, pay half on the first load and the rest on the last load. That keeps you both honest.

If you've made a deal to buy "everything" in a house, be sure to look *everywhere*. I've found many good things that were left in the garage, the attic, the shed, and the yard (front and back). Get all you can get for your money. If you're not buying "everything," you should choose an empty area of the house and put all the items you want to buy there as you select them — that way you don't forget anything and there's no confusion about what's being sold. I've had people tell me they want to sell this and that and I make the deal, then they claim they didn't say what I heard. Be very clear about what you're buying — if you have to, repeat everything the seller says before you agree to buy an item just to be sure everyone's on the same page. Better yet, write a list of everything you're buying and the price of each item, and both of you sign it. That way you can provide him a copy as a receipt and there's no grounds for dispute later on.

Of course, the owner of the house (and/or the person who's in charge of selling the goods) should be present when you're taking things out, to prevent any misunderstandings or difficulties. If that's not possible (for example, if you have to make multiple trips over several days to haul it all out), get a key from him so you can come and go as you please. However, it's best not to leave your purchases at the house for a couple days because some of the items might not be there when you get back — protect your property!

Be prepared when you come to pick up what you've bought. For small, durable items, I like to use plastic tote boxes, which you can get at office supply stores. They're easy to carry, pack, and stack. Take paper to wrap glassware, dishes, and other breakable items; you can buy boxes especially for transporting such items from moving companies if you want to go the extra mile. If you've bought furniture, bring moving blankets so you can wrap the items and keep them from getting scratched. Keep some big pieces of cardboard in your truck to put between glass shelving, pictures, and furniture.

BOOTH MAINTENANCE

After your booth is up and running, you can't just leave it alone indefinitely. To make the best impression on customers you need to take care of and maintain it.

Cleaning Your Booth

The more effort you put into keeping your booth clean and well organized, the more money you'll make.

Keep your booth clear of clutter. Don't let items sit on the floor. If things can be hung up, hang them. Make sure there's room for people to bring shopping carts into your booth.

Sweep or mop (depending on the type of floor) regularly. Dust when necessary. Keep all glass shelves and showcase tops clean and polished. Pick up and dispose of all the trash people leave in your booth. In fact, having a small trash can in there is a good idea if you have the room for it and it doesn't look bad — people tend to leave empty drink cups, candy wrappers, and other trash in your booth without even thinking about it, and the quicker you can get rid of that stuff the better.

Keep the shelves neat, tidy, and full. Empty space won't make you any money, and it makes your booth as a whole look bad. If you walk into your booth and see an empty space, try to fill it with something. But don't jam the items so close together that customers have a hard time looking at them.

Every week, ask yourself these questions:

1. Is my booth well lighted?
2. Is my booth clean?
3. Is my booth full of product ready for sale?
4. Can people get into my booth easily?
5. Is there anything in my booth that's damaged?
6. Is everything priced with my vendor number and the right price?
7. Would I shop here?

Downsizing

Sometimes you may decide you've got too many booths, or have too much stuff in your booth, and that you need to downsize. You can lose money doing this if you're not careful. If you want to downsize, do it slowly. There are only so many displays, shelves, cabinets, and props that you can get rid of in a month. If you *have* to sell quickly, or you're too eager, you won't make as much money as you will if you can sell off things slowly... you also run the risk of flooding the market. Take advantage of the fact that new vendors come into most flea markets every month and are potential buyers for your booth fixtures and goods.

Moving Your Booth

Sometimes a flea market closes or has to move. That means you and all the other vendors have to get out by a certain deadline. This can be tough; it's harder to sell your fixtures and goods to other vendors who are also moving. But anything you sell you don't have to move, so sell what you can without cutting into your profits too much.

In this situation, the quicker you get out, the better for you. Often all you'll get is thirty days' notice (that's what the usual booth lease specifies). Don't wait for the deadline to approach, get out of there as soon as possible. This is particularly important if you have multiple booths; you can't put all that work off until the last minute.

The advice I gave above about moving items out of a house applies to moving your own items. Bring newspaper to wrap breakables; buy specialized moving boxes if necessary (though it's usually not); and so on. If you use plastic tote boxes, you can buy them in different colors to organize your move: all your Christmas items in red tote bins; all your Halloween ones in orange totes; and so forth. (Make sure everything fits in the bin and you put the lid on it; otherwise you can't stack them.) Putting labels on the outside of tote bins and boxes identifying what's in them, or just writing the contents on the box with a marker, helps a lot too when the time comes to unpack (a particularly important consideration when you know you're relocating your booth to another flea market).

Don't pack anything that's not worth moving. Chipped, cracked, or broken items you should probably just throw out. You may want to consider the same for items you've had for a very long time that simply aren't selling. Moving things costs you time, effort, and money; don't go to the trouble if you're going to end up getting rid of something anyway.

Once you've packed all your items you can decide what to do with shelves, walls, and other fixtures. Anything you know you'll want or need again you should keep (dismantle it for easy transport if necessary); anything else you should try to sell to other vendors before going to the effort of moving it. Try to get a good price for these items, but remember that part of the "price" is the time, effort, and money you'll save by not moving them.

Of course, all of this advice applies when you have to move a booth because you decide not to renew the lease, or the market refuses to renew your lease. But in that situation you may have more luck selling items and fixtures to other vendors who aren't going anywhere.

FINAL THOUGHTS

I wrote this book to give you a better understanding of what you're getting into when you set up and run a flea market booth; I hope you've enjoyed it and found it helpful. It's all based on the experiences and things I've learned during my flea market adventures; it's not just my opinions. Feel free to share the information with anyone it might help.

I hope you have as good a time being a vendor as I have. I learn things every day and am always ready to share that experience with whoever's interested. If you see me in a flea market sometime please let me know what you think of the book and what I might add to it to make it more helpful to new and prospective vendors.

Good luck, and I hope you make a million! Remember, the more you put into this business the more you'll get out of it.

CPSIA information can be obtained at www.ICGtesting.com
Printed in the USA
LVOW12s0044110614

389514LV00013B/200/P